Stans

Inside The Devotion, Stories, And Impact Behind Eminem's Most Loyal Fans

Wiley Crawford

Copyright Page

All rights reserved. No part of this publication may be reproduced, distributed, or transmitted in any form or by any means, including photocopying, recording, or other electronic or mechanical methods, without the prior written permission of the publisher, except in the case of brief quotations embodied in critical reviews and certain other noncommercial uses permitted by copyright law.

Copyright © Wiley Crawford, 2025

Disclaimer

This book is an independent work of commentary, analysis, and research inspired by the 2025 documentary Stans, directed by Steven Leckart and produced by Eminem and associated production companies. It is not authorized, endorsed, sponsored, or approved by Eminem, Shady Films, DIGA Studios, Hill District Media, Paramount+, or any other individuals or entities involved in the creation, production, or distribution of the documentary.

All names, trademarks, and copyrighted materials referenced in this book remain the property of their respective owners and are used solely for the purposes of identification, commentary, and education under the fair use provisions of applicable copyright law. While every effort has been made to ensure the accuracy and reliability of the information provided, the author and publisher make no representations or warranties, express or implied, regarding the completeness, accuracy, or suitability of the content for any purpose. Any opinions, interpretations, or conclusions expressed are solely those of the author. This book is not intended to replace the viewing of the documentary Stans, but to offer additional perspectives, insights, and context for readers who wish to explore its themes and subjects in greater depth. Readers are encouraged to consult original sources and view the documentary for their own interpretation.

The author and publisher disclaim any liability for any direct, indirect, incidental, or consequential damages arising from the use or reliance upon the information contained in this work.

Table Of Contents

Introduction

Chapter 1: The Birth Of A Word
How Stan Became More Than A Song

Chapter 2: Slim Shady's Mirror
Eminem's Career Through The Eyes Of His Fans

Chapter 3: The Making Of Stans
Behind The Camera With Steven Leckart And Eminem

Chapter 4: Stories Inked In Skin
Fans Who Wear Eminem's Words For Life

Chapter 5: Healing In The Lyrics
When Music Becomes A Lifeline

Chapter 6: From Obsession To Connection
The Fine Line Between Love And Extremes

Chapter 7: Global Stan Nation
How Eminem's Music Unites Strangers Worldwide

Chapter 8: Fame From The Other Side

Eminem On Sobriety, Fatherhood, And Fan Encounters

Chapter 9: Icons And Allies
Cameos, Collaborations, And Industry Perspectives

Chapter 10: Pop Culture Power
How Stan Changed Language And Internet Culture

Chapter 11: The Psychology Of Fandom

Chapter 12: Lessons From The Stan Effect
What Eminem And His Fans Teach Us About Identity

Conclusion

Introduction

Some songs are hits. Some songs are anthems. And then there are songs that change the language itself. When Eminem released Stan In 2000, he wasn't just telling a story about an obsessed fan he was defining a cultural archetype. In the years since, Stan has gone from a haunting narrative in a rap verse to a dictionary word, a pop-culture shorthand for deep, unwavering, and sometimes dangerous fandom. But behind the slang, behind the memes, behind the global phenomenon, there are real people living, breathing, feeling individuals whose connection to Eminem's music is as personal as it is profound.

The 2025 documentary Stans, directed by Steven Leckart and produced by Eminem himself, flips the spotlight. Instead of focusing on the artist's rise to fame, it centers the people who've walked every step of that journey alongside him not on stage, but in their hearts and lives. From tattoo-covered superfans to quiet listeners who found healing in his lyrics, these are the stories of devotion, resilience, identity, and the complicated beauty of being seen by someone you may never meet. This book dives deeper into the world Stans reveals, exploring the film's themes, unpacking its emotional moments, and tracing the fine line between admiration and obsession.

You'll meet fans who carry Eminem's words on their skin, in their journals, and in the very fabric of their identities. You'll see how a man from Detroit became a lifeline for strangers around the globe, and how those strangers, in turn, became part of his story. Here, we'll look beyond the headlines and the stereotypes, peeling back the layers of fandom to understand its power. We'll examine what it means to be part of a community bound by art, how music becomes a mirror for our struggles, and why certain voices speak so directly to our souls. Whether you've been rapping along with Lose Yourself For decades, discovered Eminem on a streaming playlist last week, or are simply curious about the human side of celebrity culture, this book invites you to step into the shoes and the hearts of the people who proudly call themselves Stans. Because in the end, this isn't just a story about Eminem. It's a story about all of us about the need to be understood, the urge to belong, and the music that makes us feel less alone.

Chapter 1: The Birth Of A Word

How Stan Became More Than A Song

In the summer of 2000, a haunting piano loop, a plaintive hook from Dido's Thank You, and a four-verse narrative turned the hip-hop world on its head. Eminem's Stan wasn't just another track on his multi-platinum album The Marshall Mathers LP it was a cinematic story in rhyme, delivered with such precision that it blurred the line between music and literature.

On the surface, the song told the fictional tale of Stan, an increasingly unstable fan who writes a series of letters to Eminem, moving from admiration to frustration to tragic desperation when he feels ignored. But beneath the fictional character was a commentary on fame, parasocial relationships, and the way artists and fans connect or fail to connect in the modern age. At the time of its release, Stan was groundbreaking because it inverted the usual fan-artist narrative. Hip-hop had long thrived on self-mythology and boasting; here was a rap song that wasn't about the artist's power but about the emotional consequences of that power on the listener. Eminem's delivery was both empathetic and unsettling, allowing listeners to feel the humanity of the fan while also recognizing the danger in obsession.

What Eminem could not have predicted was that the name Stan would leave the confines of the song and enter the everyday language of millions. Initially, stan was used informally among music fans to describe an ultra-dedicated follower, often with an edge of unhealthy obsession. By the mid-2010s, thanks in large part to the rise of internet culture and social media fandoms, stan had been stripped of its purely negative connotation and repurposed into a badge of honor. Online fan communities, especially on Twitter, Tumblr, and later TikTok, adopted the term as a way to proudly declare allegiance. I stan Beyoncé or We stan a queen became common phrases playful, hyperbolic, and celebratory. In 2017, the Oxford English Dictionary officially added stan as both a noun an overzealous or obsessive fan of a particular celebrity and a verb to be an overzealous or obsessive fan of. What began as the name of a fictional character had become part of global slang.

This evolution reflects a broader shift in fandom. The internet collapsed the distance between celebrities and their audiences, making it possible for fans to interact with or at least feel closer to their idols. In that environment, stanning transformed from a warning about obsession into a way to express love, loyalty, and belonging. Although Stan was a fictional tale, Eminem has explained in interviews that it was inspired by real fan interactions he had experienced in the early stages of his fame. The late '90s and early 2000s were a whirlwind for him going from local Detroit battle rapper to global superstar almost overnight. That meteoric rise brought floods of fan letters, some of them deeply personal and emotionally raw.

Many fans shared stories of how his music helped them through depression, abuse, or addiction. Others made extreme requests, crossed personal boundaries, or expressed troubling dependency on him as a figure of hope. Stan condensed those experiences into a single, tragic character one who starts off relatable and ends as a cautionary tale.

In creating Stan, Eminem tapped into the darker side of fame the way an artist's words can become intertwined with a fan's identity, for better or worse. That duality is part of why the song has endured. For some, it's a gripping story; for others, it's a mirror reflecting their own emotional investment in an artist's work. Directed by Dr. Dre and Philip G. Atwell, the Stan music video amplified the song's impact. British actor Devon Sawa played Stan with unnerving realism, while Dido appeared as Stan's girlfriend. The visuals tracked the narrative beat by beat: the candlelit writing sessions, the Eminem posters covering every inch of the bedroom, the gradual unraveling of Stan's mental state.

The video's stormy finale Stan driving off a bridge with his girlfriend in the trunk burned itself into the cultural memory. MTV placed it in heavy rotation, and it quickly became one of the most discussed videos of the year. The imagery not only reinforced the cautionary message but also made Stan an instantly recognizable archetype: the dangerous side of unfiltered idol worship. What's remarkable is how the term stan was reclaimed by the very communities it was meant to caution. This shift speaks to the fluid nature of language and culture. Hip-hop fans, pop fans, and internet users at large began using stan without the tragic undertones, instead making it synonymous with loyalty, enthusiasm, and pride. In the Stans documentary, this transformation is a key thread. The film captures real-life fans whose devotion mirrors Stan's intensity but with healthier, life-affirming results. There's Nikki, the Guinness World Record holder for most Eminem tattoos, whose body art is a testament to gratitude rather than obsession. There's the fan who found courage in Eminem's lyrics to come out as transgender, and another who credits the rapper's words with helping him survive grief and addiction.

These modern-day Stans are living proof that the bond between artist and audience can be profound without being destructive. The documentary reframes the idea of stanning as something that can empower and unite people rather than isolate them. Today, stan belongs to more than just Eminem's legacy; it's a fixture in the global vocabulary. K-pop fans stan BTS. Sports fans stan LeBron James. Political followers even stan candidates. The word's universality shows how Stan tapped into something deeply human: the longing to connect, to belong, and to champion someone whose voice speaks to us.

Yet the original cautionary note still lingers in the background. In the age of instant access to celebrities through social media, the boundaries between healthy admiration and unhealthy fixation can still blur. The story of Stan remains relevant as both a cultural meme and a subtle reminder of the need for perspective in fandom.

Two decades after its release, Stan is still discussed in music criticism, psychology lectures, and pop culture think pieces. Its endurance lies in its layered meaning: part gripping drama, part social commentary, part linguistic phenomenon. The Stans documentary brings this full circle. It recognizes that while the word may have shifted in tone, the emotional depth behind it remains. For some fans, Eminem's music was a soundtrack to survival. For others, it was a mirror showing them their strength. And for Eminem, those connections whether fleeting or lifelong are a testament to the reach of art.

The birth of the word stan reminds us that language is alive, evolving with each generation. But more importantly, it reminds us that music isn't just something we listen to, it's something we live with, grow with, and sometimes, define ourselves by.

Chapter 2: Slim Shady's Mirror

Eminem's Career Through The Eyes Of His Fans

When fans see Eminem, they see more than rap verses; they see pieces of themselves. Stans flips the camera, using their eyes as the lens through which we revisit Eminem's career. His trajectory from gritty Detroit beginnings to global superstardom is filtered through personal pilgrimage, devotion, and shared healing. One of the most vivid fan-guided sequences features Zolt Shady, a die-hard follower since 2001.

In a striking homage, Zolt leads the viewer through Detroit's hallowed ground battle rap stages, demolished childhood haunts, and the gritty streets that shaped Eminem's origin story. As Zolt narrates his journey from discovery to fandom, his devotion echoes earlier eras of music fandom raw, unfiltered, and deeply rooted in place rather than platform. Another fan goes even deeper documenting their devotion through body art. With 22 portraits of Eminem's face inked across their skin, this fan transforms fandom into living, breathing tribute. It's not just applause, it's permanence. This visual tells us that Eminem's influence transcends albums or lyrics; it resides in identity itself. The documentary tracks Eminem's career chronologically but it does so through fan commentary.

They follow the arc from early mixtapes and raw releases through watershed albums like The Marshall Mathers LP, Relapse, and Recovery, each phase illuminated by those who were listening closely. Industry voices like Dr. Dre, Jimmy Iovine, and even Ed Sheeran, Carson Daly, and Adam Sandler offer context, while fans anchor the narrative in lived experience. Eminem appears in the film expressing a blend of gratitude and discomfort. When fans retrace his steps visiting his former neighborhood or the demolished childhood home he admits, It's cool that people care, but it's weird because it's me. His humility clashes with the myth of celebrity, and this moment becomes a mirror for fans who see their hero and perhaps themselves exposed in that reflection. Stans doesn't shy away from the darker chapters. Scenes depicting Eminem's overdose, his grief over losing Proof, and the emotional toll of addiction are interwoven with fans' testimonies.

For many, his admissions of vulnerability became beacons of hope. One recovering addict describes how hearing Eminem's honesty gave them the strength to reach out for help. Another talks through grief with lyrics that felt made for them. This film intentionally avoids sensationalism. As Creative Collaboration notes, fans introduce themselves simply: My name is... Then they speak about Eminem as though he's more than a celebrity he's a confidant. Their loyalty isn't about celebrity worship; it's about resonance. Stans juxtaposes Eminem's public myth, the hard-charging Slim Shady persona, with the private human Marshall Mathers. This duality casts a long shadow: fans are drawn to his bravado and his vulnerability in equal measure. Industry voices like Paul Rosenberg point to that contrast as what made Eminem compelling and what, at times, made fandom precarious. Director Steven Leckart was deliberate.

A public survey received over 9,000 submissions to participate in the documentary but the film filtered out dangerously obsessive responses. What remains is a tapestry of genuine, emotionally grounded fans: a Guinness World Record holder for Eminem tattoos; a trans fan who legally adopted Marshall as a name; a teenager whose unsent letters reveal how deeply lyrics resonated. Across demographics, gender, nationality, generation fans articulate a shared emotional truth: Eminem gave them words for feelings they couldn't name. Whether battling depression, coming to terms with identity, or marking milestones like Sobriety, his music was the thread that tied their stories together. In these testimonies, his career becomes a collective lifeline. By viewing Eminem's career through fan experiences, Stans reframes the narrative. This chapter echoes a turning point: fans are no longer just observers, but co-authors of the story. Their reflections reveal how a lyrics-first artist built a legacy not just through records sold, but through hearts healed.

When Slim Shady is reflected back through the eyes of his fans, something profound happens. His catalog becomes more than music; it's the soundtrack to survival, revelation, and growth. Stans reminds us that the mirror between artist and audience is often mutual. They lifted him; he lifted them. And in that give-and-take, Eminem's story and theirs becomes unforgettable.

Chapter 3: The Making Of Stans

Behind The Camera With Steven Leckart And Eminem

The making of Stans was more than just the creation of a music documentary, it was a cultural excavation. At its core, it was a deep dive into two decades of fan devotion, controversy, and the complicated relationship between celebrity and audience. The project brought together two unique creative forces: Steven Leckart, an award-winning documentarian with a knack for telling human-centered stories, and Eminem, the notoriously private rap icon whose music inspired the very phenomenon being examined.

Leckart approached the project with his trademark investigative style. He wanted to go beyond the surface of fan culture, avoiding clichés and sensationalism. His goal was to uncover the real human experiences behind the label of Stan, a term that, thanks to Eminem's 2000 hit of the same name, has become part of the global lexicon. For Leckart, this meant months of archival research, hours of interviews, and a commitment to balancing the narrative between admiration and critique. Eminem's involvement was equally vital. While he had collaborated on documentaries before, he had never co-created one that examined the ripple effects of his own art in such detail.

Initially cautious about revisiting Stan, a track known for its dark and tragic narrative, Eminem recognized the potential of telling this story through the lens of documentary filmmaking. He was particularly interested in how the term had evolved over time from representing a fictional, obsessive fan to describing real-life individuals whose devotion could be both inspiring and alarming. The early development phase was a meticulous

25

process. Leckart and Eminem agreed that authenticity had to be the cornerstone of the film. This meant securing access to original music videos, behind-the-scenes footage, and never-before-seen materials from Eminem's archives. It also meant speaking to fans directly from those who had been inspired to create art, start careers, or change their lives because of Eminem's music, to those whose obsession had taken a darker turn.

Production began with a series of intimate interviews. Leckart's team traveled to multiple countries, capturing stories from fans who had been there since Eminem's rise in the late '90s, as well as younger followers who discovered his music years later through streaming platforms. Each interview added layers to the documentary's narrative, showing how Stan had become both a cautionary tale and a badge of honor, depending on the perspective. Eminem's role behind the camera was not just symbolic; he actively participated in shaping the narrative arc. He sat in on edit sessions, offered feedback on interview selections, and even suggested thematic sequences. His input was crucial in ensuring that the documentary did not paint fans in a single light. While the Stan archetype has often been reduced to a stereotype of dangerous obsession, the documentary presented a more complex view: fans as multifaceted individuals whose passion is tied to personal history, identity, and belonging.

Visually, Leckart opted for a mix of cinematic styles. The film blends glossy, high-definition performance clips with raw, handheld footage from fan gatherings and concerts. Archival VHS recordings from the early 2000s are interspersed with present-day interviews, creating a time-lapse effect that mirrors Eminem's career trajectory. These visual contrasts serve as reminders of how both technology and fan culture have evolved over the years.

The collaboration between Leckart and Eminem also extended to the soundtrack. Rather than relying solely on existing Eminem tracks, they incorporated remixes, alternate versions, and isolated vocal tracks that offered new textures to familiar songs. This approach gave audiences a fresh way to connect with the music while reinforcing key emotional beats in the narrative.

One of the biggest challenges in production was maintaining a balanced tone. Leckart was determined to explore the darker aspects of fandom cases where devotion tipped into unhealthy territory without sensationalizing them. Eminem, too, wanted to avoid making the film feel like an exposé. Instead, they agreed to frame these stories within broader conversations about celebrity, mental health, and the internet's role in amplifying fan behaviors. The making of Stans was also shaped by the changing nature of fan-artist interaction in the digital age. The documentary examines how social media platforms have blurred the boundaries between celebrities and their audiences. In earlier decades, fan letters and chance encounters were the main ways to connect with artists. Today, a single tweet can create an instant exchange for better or worse. Eminem himself has had a complicated relationship with this immediacy, and the documentary captures his candid reflections on both its benefits and its pitfalls.

Perhaps the most striking element of the film's production was its willingness to be self-reflective. Eminem openly addressed how Stan, a song he wrote two decades ago, has followed him throughout his career. He discussed moments when the term was used against him, how it evolved into internet slang, and how he feels about its legacy today. Leckart ensured these moments were handled with nuance, allowing viewers to see the artist not just as a cultural figure, but as someone grappling with the unintended consequences of his art. The editing process was where the vision truly came together. Leckart and his team sifted through hundreds of hours of footage, piecing together a story that was both personal and universal. They organized the film into thematic chapters, each one exploring a different facet of fandom from devotion and inspiration to obsession and boundaries. The result was a narrative that felt cohesive yet open-ended, encouraging audiences to draw their own conclusions.

By the time Stans premiered, it was clear that the documentary was more than a nostalgic look at one of Eminem's most iconic songs. It was a layered examination of human connection, filtered through the lens of music and celebrity. Behind the camera, Steven Leckart's investigative precision met Eminem's personal insight, creating a partnership that elevated the film beyond standard music documentary territory. The making of Stans demonstrates what happens when an artist and a filmmaker commit to telling a story without compromise. It's a reminder that documentaries can be as much about the people behind the camera as the ones in front of it, a creative exchange where vision, vulnerability, and truth converge to leave a lasting cultural mark.

Chapter 4: Stories Inked In Skin

Fans Who Wear Eminem's Words For Life

In the Stans documentary, the image of an Eminem portrait tattooed across flesh isn't just a striking visual it's a raw confession, a personal billboard that reads: This music changed me. Among those stories, one stands out with extraordinary clarity: Nikki Patterson from Aberdeen, Scotland, whose devotion now holds a Guinness World Record.

Nikki first encountered Stan as a teenager, a moment that would redefine her relationship with music and with herself. That initial brush with Eminem's lyrics was, by her words, life-altering. At 19, she marked that connection with a tiny, backward-faced E, a nod to Eminem's iconography that was understated yet deeply

32

meaningful. Over the years, the ink multiplied. At the time her record was verified, she had over 50 tattoos 28 of them dedicated to Eminem, and 15 were portraits of his likeness. Since then, she's added another, cementing her place in the Guinness World Records as the person with the most portrait tattoos of a single musician. But the tattoos offered more than fandom; they became a reclaiming of her body and identity. Nikki struggled with body image issues, and after her first portrait in 2017, she remembers a sudden shift: she felt proud of her skin for the first time. The tattoos became an armor of confidence.

Tattoos carry stories that help anchor people to who they are, and for many fans filmed in Stans, that's exactly the point. The ink isn't tribal or trendy, it's autobiographical. Lyrics memorialized on skin a line from Till I Collapse, maybe double as life verses. Portraits may reflect admiration, but lyrics reflect the personal impact of his

33

storytelling. These bodies are diaries, worn visibly and intentionally. Nikki isn't alone in her devotion. Viewers meet fans who take pilgrimages to Detroit, tracing the tracks where Eminem battled, rapped, and rose. They follow a shared ritual walking through the same neighborhoods, visiting the demolished childhood home, standing outside once-infamous music venues. For these fans, tattoos mirror those steps: permanent markers of personal transformation.

Others share quiet but powerful gestures: the fan who legally adopts Marshall as their first name, or the trans fan who found clarity in Eminem's lyrics, anchoring their identity in shared vulnerability. Each inked image reflects a journey emerging from grief, addiction, identity struggles, or isolation and entering a narrative of resilience. In one poignant scene, fans gather to show their ink some new, some decades old alongside peers whose faces reflect stories of healing. One woman displays lyrics inscribed across her thigh, a verse that saved her during depression. Another points to her forearm portraits evolving from shy admiration into bold, visible statements of belonging. The camera lingers on each symbol: tattoos are more than decoration; they form a map of community.

There's a tension in permanence. Tattoos never fade entirely, and that can mirror the lasting emotional weight of the fandom. For Nikki, inking Eminem's image didn't just show love it made her confront vulnerability and ownership of her story. Others hesitate, asking themselves: Can a moment of devotion become too permanent? In Stans, this reflection doesn't serve as warning; instead, it's an invitation to consider how deeply art can root within a person.

Contrast this devotion with Stan, the fictional character whose obsession ended in tragedy. Stans redeems the term not by denying its origin, but by redefining it. Nikki embodies a transformed version of fandom: one rooted in healing, not harm. Her tattoos aren't warnings carved into flesh, they're affirmations of survival and celebration. In Stans, tattoos become cultural currency, a way for fans to speak without words. When one of them smiles, revealing Eminem's face on their arm, it says everything: they've chosen to live their story visually, openly. These tattoos broadcast ownership over fandom, turning what was once dismissed as excessive into authentic expression.

In the editing room, the filmmakers layered fan interviews over closeups of tattoos ink against skin, words and portraits side by side. That visual says: these are lived stories. The juxtaposition underscores humanity: beneath every tattoo is an experience, a memory, a reason to carry this weight permanently. What emerges in this chapter is not vanity but daring devotion. Fans like

Nikki don't design their ink for viral attention; they live with it. And living with it means every glance in the mirror is a reaffirmation. The tattoos embody love that is durable, not desperate for an ongoing conversation with art, rather than a one-time reaction. The significance of these tattoos extends beyond personal expression; it offers insight into fandom's evolution. Tattoos become trackers of emotional milestones, albums that helped people through loss, lyrics that sparked identity revelation, portraits that anchor them to hope. In this way, Stans isn't just a documentary, it's a gallery of life stories linked in tribute to the artist who helped tell them.

Chapter 5: Healing In The Lyrics

When Music Becomes A Lifeline

For many people, music isn't just entertainment, it's a survival mechanism. Eminem's lyrics, raw with personal battles, sharp honesty, and unfiltered emotions, have become more than just rhymes to millions of listeners. They've served as a kind of therapy, a lifeline that helps fans navigate mental health struggles, addiction, trauma, and the daily grind of feeling misunderstood. This is not about casual fandom, it's about the kind of connection where a song doesn't just get played, it gets absorbed into someone's bloodstream.

Eminem's music resonates so deeply because it refuses to sugarcoat reality. In songs like Rock Bottom, Cleaning Out My Closet, and Beautiful, he opens up about poverty, depression, family pain, and personal demons. For fans experiencing similar struggles, these tracks are like hearing someone finally articulate what they've been unable to express themselves. Honesty validates their emotions; it tells them they're not broken beyond repair, just human.

One of the most common threads among fans who credit Eminem's music with helping them heal is the feeling of no longer being alone. Isolation can be one of the most crushing aspects of depression or hardship feeling like no one could possibly understand. But hearing Eminem rap about waking up hopeless, fighting addiction, or battling self-doubt makes listeners feel seen.

In interviews, some fans have described sitting in dark bedrooms, headphones on, finding themselves silently nodding to verses that feel ripped from their own lives. The effect isn't just emotional, it's chemical.

Hearing relatable words and emotions in music can trigger the brain's reward system, releasing dopamine and reducing feelings of loneliness. Eminem's music becomes a companion, a voice in the room that says, I've been where you are and I made it out. There are countless stories of fans who claim that certain Eminem tracks kept them alive during their darkest moments. Tracks like Not Afraid have become anthems for self-recovery, with their central message of resilience and starting over. When Eminem raps about choosing to walk away from the edge, it's more than inspiration it's proof that survival is possible.

Some fans have even written letters to Eminem explaining how a particular verse stopped them from making a fatal decision. The impact is especially strong because Eminem's own survival wasn't clean or easy; he's candid about relapses, mistakes, and ongoing battles. That authenticity carries more weight than a polished, overly optimistic message; it acknowledges the messiness of healing while still showing a way forward. For those recovering from addiction or mental health issues, music can be an anchor. Eminem's Recovery album in particular has been adopted as a personal soundtrack for people trying to rebuild their lives. Tracks like Going Through Changes speak openly about the exhausting cycle of depression and the fear of backsliding, while Cinderella Man injects the listener with determination to rewrite their own story.

Therapists and addiction counselors have even mentioned that certain clients respond strongly to music-based coping strategies, with Eminem's work often topping the list. His ability to weave vulnerability into aggressive beats creates a balance of catharsis and empowerment listeners can cry through one verse and feel ready to fight through the next. While professional help is essential, lyrics can act as a supplementary form of therapy. Many fans engage with

Eminem's words by journaling about what they mean to them, tattooing them on their bodies, or reciting them as daily affirmations. The process of internalizing these words turns them into personal mantras. Take the line I'm not afraid to take a stand from Not Afraid. For some, it's not just a catchy hook, it's a daily reminder to confront their fears, whether that's going to therapy, leaving an abusive relationship, or starting over in a new city. By repeating these lines, fans are, in essence, practicing a form of cognitive reframing turning negative thought patterns into empowering ones.

Eminem's music as a lifeline isn't limited to a particular demographic. Fans from vastly different backgrounds, teenagers in rural towns, single parents in big cities, soldiers deployed overseas find common ground in his words. His music travels across borders, connecting people who might never meet but share the same pain and the same will to overcome it. In some cases, parents and children bond over Eminem's tracks, using them as a way to talk about difficult subjects like addiction or mental illness. In others, communities come together through fan groups and online forums, offering peer-to-peer support grounded in the messages of his music. What makes Eminem's lyrics uniquely healing is the way he blends vulnerability with aggression. While many artists focus solely on one or the other, Eminem's approach mirrors the emotional reality of recovery: sometimes you need to vent, sometimes you need to fight. Songs like Till I Collapse deliver the grit to keep pushing, while tracks like Headlights encourage forgiveness and emotional release.

This duality allows fans to process both their rage and their sadness, helping them move through emotions rather than suppress them. It's a release valve one that doesn't just let out steam but also helps rebuild inner strength. The healing power of

Eminem's lyrics often extends beyond the songs themselves. His very presence as a public figure who openly discusses his mistakes, vulnerabilities, and triumphs reinforces the possibility of personal redemption. Fans see someone who was once drowning in his own vices stand on a stage sober, healthy, and still thriving creatively. That visible transformation becomes as inspiring as the music itself.

Chapter 6: From Obsession To Connection

The Fine Line Between Love And Extremes

In the world of celebrity admiration, there's a fragile line that separates genuine connection from dangerous fixation. At first glance, fandom may appear as harmless enthusiasm, a shared excitement for music, films, or public appearances. But when admiration deepens into all-consuming obsession, it can distort reality, redefine relationships, and even put lives at risk. In the context of Stans, the documentary reveals how that transition from love to extremes often happens subtly, unnoticed until it spirals beyond control.

The term Stan itself, born from a fusion of stalker and fan, captures the paradox at play. Many begin as devoted supporters, finding joy in their favorite artist's work, attending concerts, buying merchandise, and engaging in online discussions. This is the love side of the spectrum, where admiration fuels positivity, creativity, and community. For some, these shared passions create genuine friendships, emotional healing, and even personal growth. A favorite song might become a lifeline during hardship, or a public figure's resilience might inspire someone to overcome personal struggles. In such cases, fandom becomes a source of empowerment.

However, the documentary makes clear that this emotional connection can morph into something darker. The extreme side of the spectrum begins when boundaries blur when a fan's personal identity becomes inseparably tied to the object of their admiration. The celebrity is no longer a distant figure but a central force in the fan's reality. Small signs of obsession can creep in: constant monitoring of the celebrity's online activity, intense emotional reactions to their personal life decisions, and the belief that one's loyalty should be reciprocated personally. One of the most striking insights in Stans is how modern technology accelerates this shift. Social media allows unprecedented access to celebrities' private and public lives. While this can make fans feel closer than ever, it also fuels unhealthy expectations. When an artist shares a glimpse of their home or a personal thought, it can create an illusion of intimacy convincing some fans that they are entitled to more access, more answers, more acknowledgment.

The documentary doesn't just analyze the psychology of obsession; it humanizes it. It presents real-life stories where admiration crossed the line into intrusive behavior tracking movements, sending unsolicited gifts, or confronting celebrities in their private spaces. Some of these encounters ended in mere discomfort; others escalated into legal action or personal danger. These cases illustrate the extremes the title warns about, showing how quickly love can twist into control or possession. But the transformation isn't always obvious to the fans themselves. In interviews, psychologists featured in Stans explain how human brains are wired for attachment. When that attachment forms around a public figure, the brain reacts similarly to how it would in a personal relationship.

Dopamine surges during a celebrity's big moment can mimic the emotional highs of a romantic connection. Over time, the brain learns to associate happiness and self-worth with the celebrity's approval or success. This neurological loop makes it incredibly difficult for some individuals to step back and maintain perspective. On the flip side, the documentary also highlights instances where intense fandoms have created positive forms of connection. Charitable projects, fan-led mental health initiatives, and grassroots campaigns to support causes championed by celebrities show that deep admiration doesn't have to be destructive. In these cases, the bond between fan and figure becomes a force for collective good, channeling passion into tangible change. The real tension is about control and respect. Love, in its purest fan form, respects boundaries.

It celebrates the art without demanding ownership of the artist. Extremes, however, demand proximity, influence, and personal validation. The documentary's narrative makes it clear that once a fan believes they deserve a certain level of access or involvement, the relationship has shifted into dangerous territory. In the most sobering segments, Stans examines how these extremes impact celebrities themselves. The constant pressure of being under surveillance, even by well-meaning admirers, can lead to anxiety, burnout, and social withdrawal. Some public figures have had to move homes, hire security, or limit public appearances not because of overt threats, but because of the relentless expectation for closeness. The emotional toll is compounded by the knowledge that the same fans who express love can turn on them in anger or disappointment if their expectations aren't met.

The chapter's theme resonates beyond celebrity culture. It prompts viewers and by extension, readers to reflect on the boundaries in all relationships, parasocial or otherwise. Just as in friendships or romance, healthy connections require mutual respect and an understanding of personal space. When either side, especially the fan, ignores that balance, the relationship can tip into unhealthy patterns.

By the end of this section, the message is clear: admiration is not inherently harmful. In fact, it can be deeply meaningful and even life-changing. But unchecked, it can slip into obsession, eroding the humanity of the person on the pedestal. Stans doesn't condemn fandom; it warns about its potential to evolve into something unrecognizable when boundaries dissolve. The fine line between love and extremes is one we must each consciously navigate, remembering that connection thrives only when respect remains intact.

Chapter 7: Global Stan Nation

How Eminem's Music Unites Strangers Worldwide

Across continents and cultures, across languages and generations, a global community has formed around Eminem. This transcendence isn't just about streaming numbers or ticket sales, it's about the invisible bonds formed through lyrics that resonate deeply with human experiences. Stans explores this phenomenon, showing how strangers across the globe have found connection through Eminem's music and how that connection has become a lifeline.

Eminem's rise began in Detroit, but it was never destined to remain local. His music, filled with candid emotion, personal hardship, and relentless honesty, crossed oceans through mixtapes, pirated CDs, and ultimately digital platforms. Stans captures that expansion visually and emotionally following fans on personal pilgrimages, whether to Detroit streets or to concerts thousands of miles from home. Through their stories, we see how songs from a working-class neighborhood became global anthems for identity and survival.

The documentary introduces us to fans from unexpected places: a transgender person who found clarity, a fan who legally adopted Marshall as a name in tribute, and tattooed fans whose bodies serve as canvases of devotion. These individuals come from different cultural backgrounds but share one thing: Eminem's words transformed something inside them. Their voices become threads in a cultural quilt, an international tapestry of healing, resilience, and fierce pride.

Online, fans from diverse regions exchange stories. A user in Libya confesses they embraced the music before learning English, while another in Asia expresses loyalty that transcends language barriers. One voice claims pride in calling themselves a Stan, even without physical proximity or immediate understanding. These personal affirmations ground the documentary in collective nuance demonstrating that fandom is also about empathy, interpretation, and unspoken kinship across borders.

Despite vast distances, fans share rituals: listening parties, virtual karaoke covers, fan art exchanges, and hashtag campaigns. In one striking example, a New York pop-up event mirrored those global rituals in real life organizing look-alike contests, immersive fan experiences, and live gatherings that celebrate the shared culture. Stans puts these gatherings alongside personal moments, tattoo sessions, trips to Detroit, or fans whispering lyrics alone in rooms to show the full arc from private devotion to public celebration. For fans worldwide, Eminem's cadence, rhythm, and emotion demand attention, even when English isn't their first language. His rhythmic wordplay carries emotional weight that transcends literal meaning. In Stans, some fans describe discovering complex emotions, from guilt to hope, through songs that echo their own unspoken struggles. The music becomes a shared language, a conduit through which emotional storms are translated, acknowledged, and soothed.

Being a Stan evolves in the film from solo obsession to shared identity. Fans don't just say they stand, they express belonging, creating communities through social media groups, fan pages, and collaborative projects. One fan-run Twitter initiative exists to unite Stans and amplify challenges, tributes, and empathy. Their efforts transform fandom from passive admiration into active, compassionate community-building. Eminem's career spans decades, carrying listeners from adolescence into adulthood. Stans carefully weaves that personal timeline into the broader narrative. Longtime fans recall sitting in bedrooms in the early 2000s, holding mixtapes like lifelines. Younger fans describe discovering him via viral clips or streamed playlists, then diving into older catalogues to reconstruct emotional histories. That temporal transmission shows how art passed through time can connect generations turning teenage isolation into collective legacy.

Many features in Stans came to Eminem during difficult moments, relationships ended, gender transitions, grief, or mental illness. His albums were sanctuaries, his lyrics companions in darkness. The film presents clips of these stories, quiet confessions, raw voices speaking into a lens that layers into a global testimony: that fans, who once felt alone, learned they mattered because they were heard. Eminem's own interviews reflect awareness and humility. He acknowledges being moved or unsettled when fans visit sites of his youth or display their devotion physically. These encounters echo internationally: while fans across the globe trace his journey, he watches theirs. Through Stans, we see the reciprocal nature of fandom not just fans seeing Eminem, but Eminem, in small ways, seeing them back.

At the end of the day, what Stans showcases is a fandom defined by unity in diversity. A fan in one country finds accidental solace in a lyric penned thousands of miles away. Another finds identity in ink, song, or self-definition linked to a man from Detroit. Across the film, Stan's culture transforms from stereotype into global mosaic, a testament that art, when honest and unfiltered, can become a bridge across worlds.

Chapter 8: Fame From The Other Side

Eminem On Sobriety, Fatherhood, And Fan Encounters

For most of his career, Eminem's life played out like raw confessional blistering verses, unflinching interviews, and public battles with addiction, fame, and family. But the Eminem we see today is far from the chaotic figure who once fueled headlines. Eminem's road to sobriety was not just a health choice it was a survival necessity. By the mid-2000s, prescription drug abuse had taken a dangerous toll on his body and mind.

The 2007 overdose that nearly ended his life marked a turning point. In later interviews, he admitted that doctors told him he had only hours to live if he hadn't been found in time. Recovery was not instantaneous. He entered rehab multiple times, and at first, even the process felt alien. Eminem described the early days as a haze, his mind still rewiring itself after years of substance dependency. But he also credits his obsessive nature once destructive in addiction as a saving grace in recovery. He threw himself into exercise, writing, and self-education about addiction as a way to rebuild both his physical health and mental resilience.

In the years since, Eminem has been open about the challenges of staying sober, especially in an industry where temptation can appear backstage or even in the recording booth. He celebrates his sobriety milestones quietly but meaningfully, once posting a coin from a recovery program marking over a decade clean. For him, sobriety is not just about staying alive it's about living with clarity and purpose. While Eminem has written countless songs about his daughter Hailie, fatherhood became a deeper guiding force in his post-addiction life. Being a present, responsible parent was both a motivation to get clean and a constant reminder of what mattered beyond the charts. Hailie wasn't the only one Eminem also took on a paternal role for his niece Alaina and his half-brother Nathan. Balancing his career with parenting meant building boundaries. Fame may have given him wealth and influence, but in his private world, Eminem became fiercely protective of his family's privacy. This often meant keeping his children away from Hollywood events or public appearances entirely.

Interestingly, fatherhood didn't just influence his personal decisions, it reshaped his music. His post-recovery albums reflect a more measured perspective on family, moving from the rage-fueled custody battles of his early work to a tone of gratitude and pride. He still raps about his struggles, but now with an awareness of how his actions ripple through the lives of those closest to him. For someone whose career was built on being larger-than-life, Eminem has often said he feels awkward in public settings. His fame makes anonymity impossible, yet he's far from the celebrity who seeks out attention. He has spoken about the challenge of going to a restaurant or a store without being recognized, and how encounters with fans can range from deeply touching to downright overwhelming.

There are moments when fans approach him to thank him for saving their lives, sharing stories of how his music helped them through addiction, depression, or abuse. Eminem says those conversations are humbling reminders that the impact of his work goes far beyond entertainment. Yet, he also admits it can be difficult to fully respond in those moments, not because he doesn't care, but because the weight of such stories can be emotionally intense. Other times, fan encounters have been more chaotic crowds forming unexpectedly, autographs being pushed into his hands, and camera phones flashing before he can react. This unpredictability is part of what keeps Eminem's public appearances so rare. He prefers controlled environments, like meet-and-greet sessions at concerts, where he can focus entirely on those interactions without being swarmed.

Eminem's fame has always been tied to a carefully crafted persona whether it was the outrageous Slim Shady, the vulnerable Marshall Mathers, or the competitive rap titan. Post-sobriety, he's become more selective about what aspects of his life he reveals. His interviews are fewer, and his music while still personal doesn't overshare in the same raw, self-destructive way it once did.

Part of this comes from maturity. As a younger artist, Eminem seemed to treat his private life as fair game for public consumption, often turning real-life drama into chart-topping singles. Now, with a daughter who has grown into adulthood, he's more aware of the ripple effects of his words. Fame from the other side means being intentional knowing that every lyric, every interview, and every photo can be dissected by millions.

These three elements of sobriety, fatherhood, and fan encounters are not separate lanes in Eminem's life. They inform each other in powerful ways. Sobriety gave him the clarity and stability to be a better father. Fatherhood grounded him and reminded him of the life worth protecting. And his interactions with fans, especially those who share their own recovery journeys, reinforce the importance of his staying the course.

In a way, the Eminem of today is in constant dialogue with his past self. He hasn't forgotten the chaos, the self-destructive impulses, or the mistakes. But instead of being defined by them, he uses them as fuel to maintain balance. His fame now operates less like a spotlight and more like a bridge connecting him to people who see their own struggles reflected in his story. Looking at Eminem's career now, there's a sense that he has reached a rare place in celebrity culture, a place where he doesn't need constant visibility to stay relevant. His music still breaks records, his verses still ignite debate, but he no longer lives in a cycle of provocation for the sake of headlines.

From this other side of fame, he has the freedom to choose when to engage and when to retreat, when to speak and when to let the music do the talking. The same man who once poured his chaos into rhymes now uses his platform with more precision, dropping verses that carry weight not just because of skill, but because of the life experience behind them.

Chapter 9: Icons And Allies

Cameos, Collaborations, And Industry Perspectives

Cameos in documentaries operate differently than in scripted films. They're not just about celebrity surprise; they are carefully chosen appearances meant to highlight influence, admiration, or a direct personal connection. In this documentary, the cameos serve as narrative anchors, marking pivotal moments in the subject's journey. Whether it's a quick recollection from a music legend, a heartfelt reflection from a family member, or an emotional scene involving an old friend, these appearances create small but impactful emotional peaks throughout the film.

One striking element of the cameos here is their range. You see industry icons with decades of experience, rising stars who were inspired by the subject's work, and even unlikely figures whose paths crossed in ways that shaped careers. Each cameo adds a shade of personality, sometimes humorous, sometimes sobering but always authentic. If the cameos give us the face-to-face emotional connection, the collaborations tell the story of professional synergy. Many of the documentary's most engaging moments come from revisiting collaborative projects, studio sessions, live performances, or shared advocacy work.

The film doesn't just mention these collaborations in passing. It allows us to watch them unfold, often through rare behind-the-scenes footage. You see creative friction turning into breakthroughs, unexpected pairings that produced iconic moments, and the quiet trust between collaborators that can't be faked. This is where the documentary excels: showing that no matter how remarkable an individual is, their greatest impact often happens in partnership with others. Some collaborations in the film were fleeting but explosive one-time performances that made cultural waves. Others were long-term, almost familial relationships that endured through changes in the industry. The documentary shows how these alliances not only shaped the subject's career but also influenced the careers of those they worked with.

The documentary also benefits from the voices of industry insiders who contextualize the subject's place in a broader landscape. Music critics, cultural historians, producers, and fellow artists provide a chorus of perspectives that stretch the narrative beyond biography into cultural history. These voices explain why certain creative decisions mattered, how the subject broke norms or reinforced traditions, and how the industry evolved alongside them. Sometimes, their observations are analytical, breaking down the technical craft; other times, they are deeply personal, recalling the human side of working with a driven, influential figure. One notable feature is how the documentary avoids making these interviews feel like detached commentary. Instead, the filmmakers weave them into the main story, often cutting between expert insight and visual evidence, ensuring that each point lands with clarity.

One of the most compelling threads in this chapter is the ripple effect the way the subject's work has inspired others across generations. In candid interviews, younger artists speak openly about how they discovered the subject's work, why it resonated with them, and how it shaped their own approach to art and life. This multi-generational dialogue not only reinforces the subject's legacy but also gives the audience a sense of continuity. It's not just a story about what happened in the past, it's about the living, evolving influence that still shapes the present. While cameos and collaborations can easily become scattered moments, the filmmakers here give them purpose. Every appearance, every shared memory, and every collaboration is positioned to either reveal something new about the subject or to highlight a broader truth about the industry. The pacing is deliberate; big names appear when their stories can amplify the emotional or thematic arc of the documentary.

This is why the film never feels like it's leaning on celebrity power for the sake of attention. Instead, it uses these moments to deepen the viewer's emotional investment, to make the central figure more human, and to show that their story exists within a complex network of relationships. Some of the chapter's most touching scenes happen when an ally or collaborator reflects on the last time they saw the subject. There's a tenderness in these recollections, a mix of joy for what they achieved together and sadness for moments that can't be repeated.

In one particularly memorable sequence, archival footage of a joint performance plays over an emotional interview with a fellow artist, creating a layered effect where memory and reality blur. The result is a scene that lingers long after it ends, perfectly illustrating how art, relationships, and time intertwine. Another significant aspect of the collaborations featured is their cross-cultural nature. The documentary shows how the subject often stepped beyond their comfort zone to work with people from different backgrounds, genres, and perspectives. These partnerships didn't just produce creative work, they built bridges, challenged stereotypes, and expanded audiences.

This willingness to collaborate across boundaries is framed as one of the subject's defining qualities, showing that their career was as much about connection as it was about personal achievement. As the chapter closes, the film leaves us with a clear impression: the subject's allies were more than supporting characters; they were co-authors of a legacy. Every cameo appearance, every collaborative effort, and every shared stage was a brick in the structure of their enduring influence. The message is subtle but powerful: greatness is rarely a solo act. It's a shared journey, enriched by those who walk alongside you, challenge you, and believe in your vision. In celebrating the icons and allies, the documentary also celebrates the community that made the story possible.

Chapter 10: Pop Culture Power

How Stan Changed Language And Internet Culture

When Stan first dropped, it resonated as a dark, emotional narrative about fame's unintended consequences. But beyond its chilling story, the name Stan began to take on a life of its own. It was a simple choice by Eminem, a name that rhymed with fans yet it became a linguistic landmark. Stan didn't just win awards and accolades as a song; it leapt from the Marshall Mathers LP into everyday conversations and eventually the Oxford English Dictionary, recognized officially not just as a noun but also as a verb.

In the years after Stan's release, especially with rising meme culture and social media, stan escaped its ominous origin. Online platforms like Twitter, Tumblr, and later

TikTok and Instagram turned stanning into a verb of devotion I stan, meaning I enthusiastically support. These weren't always about unhealthy obsession; they became expressions of loyalty and shared identity. That massive shift from obsessive warning to celebratory recalibration epitomizes how language adapts to cultural tides. Stan paved the way for fandom to become a form of expression, particularly online. Stan communities evolved into generative engines for memes, viral campaigns, and cultural commentary.

A stan might launch a hashtag, produce fan edits, or mock the absurdity of celebrity moments all as badges of love and humor. This meme economy transformed fandom from passive consumption into active cultural engineering, where fans dictate what's trending, who gets attention, and how moments get remembered. At the heart of this transformation sits Stan Twitter: a subculture defined by inside jokes, fervent threads, and a language all its own. From reaction GIFs to fan campaigns, it's where stanning became collaborative performance. But this space has its complexities. The same rapid mobilization that elevates fandom can also enforce toxic ambushes or cancel squads. The documentary Stans explores this duality celebrating how emotional connection can unite strangers across borders, while also recognizing how digitized devotion can spiral into expectation.

Gen Z took stan-ning even further. It's passionate, yes but often self-aware, even ironic. Stanning became a way to both uplift an artist and wink at one's own commitment to performative fandom. Fans cheer loudly, but sometimes just to mock the very idea of celebrity obsession. Through satire and sincerity, they created an ironic pop-culture commentary that keeps fandom fun but reflexive. These communities also leverage their power for activism, fundraising, and narrative shaping. From viral support during cultural movements to organized responses when their favorite artist faces criticism, stan communities blend fandom with cultural agency in unprecedented ways. Culturally, the term stan has outgrown its origin while still retaining echoes of its obsessive roots, it now reflects loyalty, cultural awareness, and online citizenship. It's a shorthand for belonging: you don't just like; you stan. This small term has shaped how we talk about fandom, identity, and digital camaraderie in the 21st century.

In the documentary Stans, that language shift is at the center. What began as a fictional, unsettling story becomes a lens to examine how fandom can be deeply human, personal, and restorative. Fans who found solace, identity, or healing through Eminem's words are briefly given the mic. Their stories remind us that stanning is not just an embrace it can be a lifeline. On one hand, stan culture is a testament to the power of shared emotion: communities formed around empathy, creativity, and mutual support. On the other, it can blur lines between admiration and entitlement, mocking and obsession. The term stan encapsulates this tension, the fine line between connection and collision. Stans captures that tension honestly, walking the same line it defines.

Chapter 11: The Psychology Of Fandom

Fandom is far more than simply liking an artist, actor, athlete, or fictional character; it's a complex psychological and social phenomenon that shapes identities, communities, and even behavior. To understand why we idolize, we have to explore the deep psychological needs fandom fulfills and how those attachments influence the way we see ourselves and the world.

Humans are wired to form attachments. From childhood, we look for figures who inspire, guide, or protect us parents, teachers, mentors. As we grow, those figures often expand into the public sphere: a singer who voices our feelings, an actor whose roles embody our dreams, or an athlete who personifies determination. Psychologists suggest that celebrity worship stems from parasocial relationships, one-sided emotional bonds where a fan feels deeply connected to someone they've never met. While the celebrity may not even know the fan exists, the fan experiences genuine feelings of closeness. These relationships aren't inherently unhealthy; in fact, they often meet the same psychological needs as real-life connections: belonging, validation, and inspiration.

Idolization often thrives on emotion. Fans turn to their idols during life's highs and lows because the connection feels safe and consistent. A favorite song might become a coping mechanism after a breakup; a sports star's comeback might motivate someone to push through personal setbacks. These emotional ties are powerful because they activate the brain's reward system. Seeing, hearing, or even thinking about a beloved figure can release dopamine, the same chemical that drives feelings of pleasure and satisfaction. That's why certain fans can recall the exact moment they first fell for an idol, almost like remembering the start of a romantic relationship. Fandom also plays a central role in identity formation. Especially during adolescence, a time when self-concept is still developing, fans often incorporate aspects of their idols into their own identities. A teenager who admires a socially conscious artist might adopt similar views and become more outspoken about causes. Someone who connects with an actor's portrayal of a brave character might feel emboldened to act more confidently in real life.

These influences can be subtle or transformative, shaping the clothes we wear, the slang we use, the values we prioritize, and the way we interact with others. Idolization rarely happens in isolation. Fans seek out others who share their passion, forming communities that can be as tight-knit as family. Whether it's a decades-old fan club, an online forum, or a social media hashtag, these spaces provide a sense of belonging. Community amplifies the experience of fandom. Shared rituals streaming an album together at midnight, attending conventions, or creating fan art strengthen bonds between members. Sociologists note that these interactions often mimic religious gatherings, with shared language, symbols, and pilgrimage events like concerts or meet-and-greets. While fandom can be a positive force, it also has a shadow side. When admiration crosses into obsession, it can distort perspectives and blur boundaries.

Fans might idealize their idols to the point of ignoring flaws or justifying problematic behavior. This can lead to cognitive dissonance, where a fan struggles to reconcile their values with their idol's actions. In extreme cases, idolization can become celebrity worship syndrome, a condition linked to unhealthy levels of attachment. These fans might feel a sense of personal betrayal over small disappointments, lash out at critics online, or even stalk the celebrity behavior that shifts from admiration to intrusion. The digital age has supercharged the psychology of fandom. Platforms like Twitter X, Instagram, TikTok, and YouTube allow fans to follow their idols' daily lives in real time. This constant stream of personal updates blurs the line between public and private, creating the illusion of intimacy.

Fans might feel they know an artist because they've seen their breakfast in an Instagram Story or watched them livestream from a dressing room. This increased access can deepen emotional investment, but it also raises expectations for constant interaction and authenticity from celebrity pressure that can be exhausting for public figures.

At its healthiest, idolization can inspire self-improvement. Fans often credit their idols with pushing them to pursue education, develop talents, or overcome personal struggles. Seeing someone achieve against the odds can act as a blueprint for personal success. For example, a fan who knows their favorite actor faced years of rejection before landing a breakthrough role might persevere through career setbacks. Similarly, a musician's openness about mental health can encourage fans to seek therapy or speak openly about their struggles.

Life can be unpredictable, stressful, and at times overwhelming. Fandom offers an escape from a controlled world where joy, passion, and connection are readily available. Watching a concert video after a bad day, binge-reading interviews, or rewatching a beloved movie can be a safe retreat from real-world pressures.

Psychologists link this to the transportation effect, where people become mentally transported into a narrative or world, temporarily distancing themselves from their problems. This escapism is not inherently negative; in moderation, it can provide relief and renewal. Idols often leave a permanent mark on who we become. Even if fandom fades over time, the lessons, values, and confidence gained through idolization can endure for years. Many adults can trace aspects of their personality, career choices, or worldview back to the influence of a celebrity they admired in their youth.

This lingering impact shows that fandom is not a fleeting hobby, it's a formative experience that weaves itself into our personal narrative. The key to healthy idolization is balance. It's possible to be deeply inspired by someone without losing perspective on their humanity. Recognizing that idols are flawed individuals, just like anyone else, allows fans to maintain respect without placing unrealistic expectations on them. Healthy fandom celebrates connection, creativity, and community while allowing space for individuality. It's about drawing strength from someone else's journey while still authoring your own.

Chapter 12: Lessons From The Stan Effect

What Eminem And His Fans Teach Us About Identity

The story of Stan is more than a cautionary tale of obsession; it's a mirror reflecting how our identities are shaped by the figures we admire and the communities we join. Eminem's fictional fan in the 2000 hit song Stan became a cultural symbol of dangerous devotion, but the phenomenon it describes extends far beyond one artist or one era. By looking closely at Eminem's career, his relationship with fans, and the lasting cultural impact of the Stan Effect, we can understand how identity is both constructed and influenced through celebrity worship, music, and belonging. For many fans, Eminem's music is more than entertainment; it's a toolkit for building personal identity. From The Slim Shady LP to The Marshall Mathers LP and beyond, his lyrics address themes like poverty, dysfunctional family life, addiction, ambition, and defiance. Fans often find parallels between their own struggles and his narratives, which allows them to adopt pieces of his worldview into their own sense of self.

The Stan Effect thrives on this process: when a fan feels the artist speaks directly to them, the line between personal experience and artistic expression blurs. Eminem's willingness to share his flaws, mistakes, and insecurities invites listeners to see themselves in him not as a distant celebrity, but as a relatable human being. For some, this connection fosters resilience, self-expression, and confidence. For others, it creates a dependency on the artist's validation, as though their identity hinges on the artist's approval or attention. Eminem's relatability is a double-edged sword. On one hand, it has built a fiercely loyal fanbase that spans decades. On the other, it has fueled cases of extreme parasocial attachment where fans feel they know the artist intimately, despite the relationship being one-sided. Stan was a dramatization of this very danger: the fictional fan, feeling unseen and unacknowledged, spirals into destructive behavior. While exaggerated, it underscored a psychological truth: when a large part of someone's self-worth comes from an idolized figure, any perceived rejection or disconnection can feel like a personal crisis.

The lesson here is balance. Admiration can inspire growth, but it must be tempered by self-awareness and the understanding that public figures are not personal saviors. The Stan Effect doesn't just occur in isolation it thrives in groups. Eminem's fans, especially in the early 2000s, built communities around shared admiration for his music and message. In fan forums, concert crowds, and later on social media, they reinforced each other's identity as part of Eminem's people. Being a Stan became a badge of belonging. This collective identity provided emotional benefits: acceptance, validation, and shared purpose. It also shaped how individuals presented themselves to the outside world, from adopting certain slang and style choices to defending Eminem in debates.

However, group identity can also become insular, breeding echo chambers where criticism of the artist is seen as betrayal. When identity is too tightly tied to a celebrity, it can hinder personal growth and openness to differing perspectives. One of the most fascinating lessons from the Stan Effect is how quickly a fictional character became a linguistic and cultural archetype. Within years, Stan entered everyday language as a verb to stan or noun a stan, describing passionate sometimes extreme fandom. This shift shows how art can directly shape cultural identity. The term stan is now used far beyond Eminem's fanbase, applying to followers of pop stars, athletes, influencers, and even brands. The identity of a stan is not just about loyalty it's about the intensity of that loyalty and the lengths one is willing to go in expressing it. Perhaps the most crucial lesson from Eminem's fan culture is the need for autonomy in identity-building. Artists can inspire, but they cannot live life for their fans. Healthy fandom recognizes the difference between being influenced and being defined by someone else.

Eminem himself has addressed this in interviews, often reminding fans that his songs reflect his own life and are not meant to be blueprints for theirs. In Stan, his closing verse essentially tells the fan to seek help and perspective, not validation from a celebrity. This sentiment remains a timeless guide for any admirer: take the inspiration, but live your own story. Eminem's career trajectory offers another insight fans' identities can evolve alongside the artist. As he moved from his rebellious early years into a more reflective and sober stage of life, some fans followed suit. They saw in his growth a model for overcoming personal demons and maturing without losing authenticity. For fans who began listening as teenagers, their connection to Eminem often matured as they aged. This adaptability shows that fandom doesn't have to be static; it can shift in ways that enrich both the fan's life and their appreciation of the artist.

Social media has supercharged the Stan Effect. Platforms like Twitter, TikTok, and Instagram allow fans to interact with their idols or at least feel closer to them more than ever before. Memes, lyric breakdowns, reaction videos, and fan art circulate constantly, reinforcing a shared identity and keeping the emotional connection alive. But this constant connection also heightens the risk of over-identification. The same tools that foster community can also trap fans in a cycle of comparison, craving, and dependency on the artist's online presence. The digital world magnifies both the positive and negative aspects of fandom identity. The final lesson from the Stan Effect is self-reflection. Healthy fans regularly ask themselves: Why does this artist resonate with me so deeply? Am I using their work to grow, or to avoid confronting my own challenges? Would I still feel whole if this artist stopped making music tomorrow?

By engaging in honest self-assessment, fans can ensure their admiration remains empowering rather than consuming. It's about keeping the artist as a source of inspiration not the foundation of one's identity.

Conclusion

The Stans documentary leaves us with more than just an inside look into one of music's most passionate and polarizing fan cultures. It serves as a mirror, reflecting how deeply music can embed itself into identity, community, and even personal purpose. Eminem's journey from battle rap corners in Detroit to becoming a global icon is impressive enough, but Stans shows us that his influence extends far beyond his lyrics; it's woven into the lives of millions who see themselves in his struggles, triumphs, and unapologetic authenticity.

Through raw interviews, archival footage, and unfiltered fan perspectives, the documentary explores the thin line between admiration and obsession, shedding light on both the empowering and unsettling sides of the Stan phenomenon. It teaches us that identity is not built in isolation; it's shaped by the voices we choose to let in, the art we cling to, and the communities we claim as our own. The Stan effect is about more than wearing merch or memorizing every lyric; it's about finding validation, belonging, and self-expression in a shared cultural language. At its best, it's a testament to the power of art to heal, inspire, and connect. At its worst, it's a cautionary tale about losing oneself in the shadow of someone else's narrative.

Eminem may have unintentionally sparked this cultural wave, but his fans have kept it alive evolving it from a song into a global identity marker. And in that transformation lies the most powerful lesson: music doesn't just tell a story it becomes part of yours. The Stans documentary doesn't close the book on this phenomenon; it hands the pen back to the fans. Whether you're a casual listener, a devoted follower, or someone who simply marvels at the psychology of fandom, the legacy of the Stan effect challenges you to ask: When you sing along, whose story are you telling and where does yours begin?

Manufactured by Amazon.ca
Acheson, AB

31119567R00052